MW00777592

"Dr. Martin has concisely laid out a roadmap to a healthy marriage, but I'd argue there are also many elements here—the instruction to be honest, patient, chivalrous, and selfless—that are necessary for healthy friendships, families, and even businesses. There's something here for everyone."

— Jason Reynolds, New York Times Best Selling Author and Public Figure

"In an era where everyone has empty opinions, this was a refreshing and honest read. I've had the pleasure of knowing April for 20 years and I've seen her practice these secrets in her relationship and later her marriage. Given her experience, this guide should really help people understand their needs and their partners needs and how to problem solve together."

— Darrell Ashwood, Podcaster

"If you're going to take any advice about marriage and how to make it work, take it from someone who's successful at it. Dr. April Martin gives it all to us in a very witty, yet very important way. I definitely took notes."

— Sunni, Radio Personality and Public Figure

"*46 Secrets to a Successful Marriage* is a real talk 101 for soon to be and married couples. Dr. April Martin's fresh take makes you feel like you are talking with a friend and not someone talking at you. For women and men alike, it shares a number of valuable insights and lessons. For the ladies there is everything from the importance of communication and compromise to keeping it sexy and the need for space for your husband. And for the men the significance of what things like listening, being honest along with supporting her dreams and passions. *46 Secrets to a Successful Marriage* is a useful tool in navigating a couples way to and through a successful marriage."

— India Sweetney, Author

46 Secrets to a
Successful Marriage:

The Truth About What
Men and Women Really Want

By: Dr. April V. Martin

© Copyright 2019 Dr. April V. Martin

ISBN 978-1-63393-852-6

Published by

 köehlerbooks™

210 60th Street
Virginia Beach, VA 23451
800–435–4811
www.koehlerbooks.com

46

Secrets
to a
Successful
Marriage

THE TRUTH
ABOUT WHAT
MEN AND WOMEN
REALLY WANT

Dr. April V. Martin

VIRGINIA BEACH
CAPE CHARLES

Table of Contents

Preface

As an African-American woman, I was born with two strikes against me: being an African-American and being a woman. Not only were those stripes shown upon my face every time I stepped into the world, but other things cast me out. A few myths that tend to stand out is that African-American women are angry all of the time, and we can't keep our men happy. That's why they leave to be with women of other races, and that's why we can't have a successful relationship or marriage. This stigma has created a pretense within our generations. This cycle is continuous because the stories of excellence that some of us have, the stories of success, happiness, satisfaction, and joy, are usually overshadowed by negativity. This story is not just about being an African-American woman in a successful marriage and defying the odds; it's about being a married woman, regardless of race, ethnicity, and age. Women are bearing a load that is much easier to carry with a man by her side. A lot of women have desired to be married since they were little girls.

According to the American Psychological Association (APA) on Divorce & Marriage, "40–50% of marriages end in divorce, and this is even higher in subsequent marriages." New studies say divorce is decreasing, but why is that? It's because people are not getting married anymore. The new generation of millennials no longer believe in the institution of marriage, and that's because everyone around them is divorcing. Marriages are said to only last on average eight years before divorcing. So in their mind, why waste eight years of your life only to end in divorce? Well, according to some articles I'm a millennial and according to other's I'm a part of Generation X, but either way, I come to you as a woman who is in a successful marriage, happy and fulfilled! I never allowed any statistic to scare me away from marriage, and believe it or not, there are still good men and women out there. By following the secrets mentioned in this book, maybe you can find love and have a successful marriage!

So this book may not be based on research like so many other books based on marriage are; rather, this book is based on real-life experience and in life, experience is just as important as statistics. Enjoy!

Dedication

I would first like to thank God for blessing me with the gift of endless energy! This book is dedicated to my father (Rest in Paradise). Thank you for always motivating, pushing and encouraging me to be more than average. Thank you for loving me throughout my unlovable years and staying dedicated to my being. I miss you, and even in paradise, you continue to motivate me. I love you.

My husband and three beautiful daughters, thank you. Thank you for understanding when I couldn't participate in a few movie nights because I had work to do. All of the late nights and early mornings were for you. I love you all!

My mom and brothers, thank you for being my strength and my rock during the most difficult time of my life. When you've lived in loyalty your entire life, you begin to see just how disloyal the world is.

1

Pray For Him

How essential is this? Pray for him. That is why this was placed first. This should be the foundation for any marriage. Pray for strength for him. Pray for peace for him. Pray for obedience for him. You can pray for anything positive you want to pray for him because praying for him to go to hell is not it. Praying for him and praying together deepens the bond the two of you share. Pray to whomever you pray to, but cover him with prayers. And do not only pray for him, but pray for his goals, his drive to work, his upcoming project, anything positive you can think of, because our men need it. They need to know you care on a higher level. When you can bond spiritually, you see a different kind of maturation in that person and the relationship.

Prayer is vital whether it's for him, you, or the relationship. Pray for a shield over the family. Pray he has the patience he needs throughout the day. Pray he is happy, satisfied, and fulfilled. Pray he feels loved and doesn't feel or succumb to the pressures of the world. When you pray for him, let him know you pray for him because he should be praying for you as well. Ask him to pray with you sometimes so he can hear it and feel it because a relationship built on God first will add an immense amount of strength to it. You don't have to be a religious and righteous person to pray for your spouse. You don't have to know every book and verse in the Bible. You can pray to whomever you pray too. You don't have to go to church every Sunday; you just have to believe, truly believe in your heart, and desire the things you ask for. This is the essential part of a marriage, and everything else follows behind it. This should be done before marriage and throughout it.

2

Talk About it

Communication is essential in any relationship. Whether it's a familial relationship, platonic relationship, or romantic relationship, talking things out makes a huge difference. I know we've heard it from our men a million times, "I'm not a mind reader!" Well, ladies, believe it or not . . . they're not! Men are simple; women are complex. We can read between the lines, and we have women's intuition, whereas men are straight to the point and direct. So, communicate to them in this manner. This way they get it, and there is no confusion. A conversation with a lot of "fluff" will lose them. Tell them exactly what it is you need to say, regardless of how they may respond, because then they can't say they didn't know or didn't understand. Expressing your needs directly and not indirectly will ensure they completely understand where you're coming from.

As women, we can't hint around about wanting to spend some quality time with them and then they say, "I'm about to go hang with my boys, I'll see you later," and then we get mad because he should've gotten the hint that we wanted to stay in and chill simply because we kept rubbing his arm, or we made a special meal and poured him a glass of wine, and we have on our boy shorts and a tank top and slow jams playing in the background. He's a man! So he'll eat the meal, drink the wine, look at you seductively and make love to you right then and there, and then kiss you on the lips and say he'll be back. Now you're upset when all you had to say was, "Hey, babes, why don't we stay in tonight, watch a movie, and chill? I want to spend some time with you, and I'll also cook your favorite meal."

Communicating about your dislikes is just as important as communicating about what you do like. In any relationship, you're always learning about your partner. You can be with them for years, but people change as they age and truly begin to become themselves and we each either learn to adapt to the person and grow, or we grow apart because you don't like the person they're becoming. So if there is something you don't like that they do, first ask yourself, "Can I live with this?" Relationships are about compromise, and there will be things your partner does that you just don't like. But is it really worth the argument and time and possibly not talking if you mention this to him? So you have to know if this behavior is something you can tolerate. Can you tolerate him being a little messy and leaving his shirt on the banister every day when he gets home from work, so you find yourself always having to move it because it looks tacky there? Is this worth an argument? Is this so bad that you can't be with him anymore? For some, it may be the breaking point. Others may just move it every single day of their lives. So, speak on it if it is something that you can't live or deal with. I always say, if you're passionate about it and you get that hot feeling inside because you're so upset and you can't get it out of your mind because it's bothering you that much, then speak on it. If you get upset for a second and then your mind drifts to something else, it's probably not that big of a deal to you.

3

Always be Accessible

What does always be accessible mean? Exactly what it says, always be accessible to your man . . . sexually! That's right . . . always! When your man wants to have sex, give it to him. I can't understand why a woman thinks withholding sex from a man as a form of punishment will make him straighten up. He'll just go elsewhere and get it if you keep withholding it. Women tend to think this is an effective way of punishing him for something he did or didn't do. Now, don't get me wrong: if your man did something like had an affair, and you found out, then no, he can't come home and make love to you, although makeup sex and mad sex is great! But withholding sex just because you-all had a small argument and you're in your feelings about it is not right. You are his wife, and he is your husband, and you-all belong to one another. So telling him no is not going to cut it. It doesn't matter how tired you are. Yes, you had to get the kids ready for school, then yourself, then you went to work, and then you got home and cooked dinner and made lunches and reviewed homework and ironed clothes and read books to the kids and put the kids to bed and then showered and you finally lay down from an exhausting day that you have to repeat tomorrow and he begins spooning you . . . you know what he wants next. You better find some source of energy and turn over to please him. You don't have to be an acrobat, because yes, you're tired, but allowing him access won't hurt, and I'm sure within five minutes all tiredness will leave your body and pleasure will overcome you.

So I'm going to be as blunt as I can be. Denying your man accessibility will slowly begin to push him into the arms of another woman. Men need to release and in most households more so than the woman. He'll appreciate it, and frequent lovemaking helps keep a relationship healthy. People tend to always name the same things as being an essential part of marriage, such as communication, loyalty, and honesty, but people seldom want to discuss just how important sex is in a marriage. So whether it's the man or the woman who has a higher sexual appetite, you need to be accessible to your spouse whenever they need it.

4

Let Him Lead

We are in an era where women are becoming more independent, women are fighting for equality, and women are handling their business by excelling academically and taking the entrepreneur world by storm. This excites me because we're able to multitask and wear a million hats. We can fulfil our dreams and still maintain the household, but somewhere along the way, a misconception arose from all of the independence. Somehow, women started feeling like they were the head of the household because their paychecks were bigger. Or that they ran things because they were able to pay their own bills and take care of themselves. Trust me when I say I love an independent woman! I love seeing my friends handle their business and achieve that degree or open that business or receive that next government grant, but we're still women and our job is not to lead in the household, it's to follow. Yes . . . follow. I know this is a hard pill for some to swallow and truth be told, it was for me as well. Being an independent, financially capable, strong woman myself, in my youth, I used to say I was the boss. Follow who? I was never a follower, and I most certainly was not going to follow a man . . . why should I? I was a natural-born leader. But as I matured, I quickly learned my role and how to manage both sides of it. Women were made to follow their man. He's the king of the house. Now, we all know that a woman makes that house a home, but a man runs it and ensures it stands and stands strong. A man should always feel peace in his home. When he comes home, he should be greeted with a kiss, asked how his day went and left alone for a few minutes. But he should always feel like the king of his castle, especially in the presence of company. I've seen women belittle their men in front of people. I know sometimes it's hard not to act out when you've just received some disturbing news or you and him are not speaking, but taking him away from the crowd and then discussing it with him is a much better approach. It'll be even better if you can wait until the company leaves, but if not, I get it. But you never want to emasculate him. Men are egotistical creatures and allowing him to lead will stroke his ego. Even if you run the relationship and everyone knows it, you never say it, and you always make sure he appears as the leader and the king. Think about it, when you dance with a man, he is supposed to lead. He is supposed to guide your waist in the direction he wants you to go and you are supposed to follow his lead, not step on his toes!

5

Compliment Him

Compliment him is meant two ways. Compliment him by adoring him and showing your appreciation towards him. And also compliment him when you're in public, you know, match his fly. Just because he's a man and men may not be as emotional as we are, doesn't mean he doesn't like to be complimented . . . Again, ladies . . . stroke his ego! I mean, you should mean it if you're going to compliment him, but a lot of times, women look at their men and in their heads, we're like, "damn he fine" or "he smells so good," yet we don't tell them. Why is that? They're human, and as humans, we like to know we're looking good by our spouse because it lets us know we're still desired . . . So compliment him. Let him know you're still attracted to him because these things will keep him home, and if he still doesn't want to stay home, best believe that if you do these twenty-three things, he will most certainly think twice before acting up, and hesitation can save marriages.

Part two of this is that you can't be going out in public with your man looking good and you looking like trash. I'm the first to say it's cute when we throw on our sweatpants, tennis shoes and throw our hair in a ponytail with no makeup on, and to be honest, men love the natural, chill look. But there's a time and place for that. My mom always told me, "Always look your best because you never know who you will run into." So when you're just going to Safeway, make sure you look good. When you're not with your man you're a reflection of him, and you don't want his boys seeing you, or better yet his ex-girlfriend, when you look a mess. So when you-all are out together, match his fly. You ever see a couple and be like, "Why the hell is he with her?" Well, don't be that couple and the girl people are looking at like, "How did she get him?" When you-all step out, you both should be stopping traffic. You should look like you two belong together. He should look at you before you-all leave the house in awe and you should look at him the same way.

6

Approach With Caution

Now, this rule is essential . . . always be mindful of how you approach him about a situation. Approaching him with your face frowned and your eyebrow raised will immediately make him defensive, and therefore the "discussion" will start as an argument because your approach was inaccurate. There's a difference between arguing and having a discussion. When you have a discussion, your face isn't distorted, and your voice isn't raised. You provide suggestions, not demands. Then, you provide reasoning as to why you feel this way and why you would suggest for him to do something so he can clearly understand your thought process. He would be more willing to listen, he won't lose interest, and he will more than likely agree to the terms. Now, when you approach him with a raised voice, or a raised eyebrow or a distorted look on your face, his guards are immediately up, and the discussion, without your knowledge, is going to begin as an argument. Then you won't get anything you wanted to accomplish from the discussion, and both of you will be yelling over one another, unable to hear what the other person is saying, and then he's tuning you out. Pointless. . . now you-all aren't talking for days and each day is spent replaying the scenario over and over in your head and pointing the blame and saying, "Well, he's wrong, so he should come to me and apologize." It's time wasted for no reason. Your approach with a man is everything. Don't get it twisted: there are going to be times when you found something out for which there is no such thing as a good approach. I get it, and it's okay, we're not perfect, simply imperfect humans trying to do right, but if that's not the case, then be mindful of how you start a discussion with him. Another suggestion is letting him know ahead of time that you'd like to talk. This way, he can prepare himself, and this will lessen the chance of him being in a bad mood when you approach him. It also gives him an opportunity to let you know in advance if he does happen to be in a bad mood, that now is not a good time to talk and you-all can speak at a later day or time. This will take time getting used to, and it's very likely the first few discussions with your husband may still go left, but you can always try again to approach him sensibly with the next discussion.

7

Stay Sexy

This should be known: your man doesn't want to be married to a frumpy woman! What's the definition of frumpy, you ask? According to the dictionary, frumpy means old-fashioned or unfashionable. In other words, boring, dull, you can't dress, and you have no sex appeal. Every man loves it when he has eye candy on his arm. When you-all go out, he sees all of the stares, and guess what . . . you belong ALL to him! There's a way to be sexy and not let it all hang out . . . you have to leave some up to the imagination . . . you know, like the sundresses men love to see women wear. Why is that? We all know why that is . . . but let's say it's also because she's not overly exposing her body, yet through the dress, you can see her silhouette and his imagination goes wild!

Also, staying sexy means doing sexy things, like surprising him with lingerie on once in a while. I know we love to go to bed comfortable, with some leggings or yoga pants with a hole or two in them and a big t-shirt that probably belongs to him. But taking off that bonnet, letting that top bun down, and putting on something sexy will make him remember one of the reasons why he married you in the first place. I know . . . yes, we're comfortable, and yes, you've been together for years now, and this is you. But once in a while, switch it up. If you don't want to do the lingerie, then wear some cute boy shorts and a tank top with no bra. Or simply wear a sexy bra and panty set to bed (although you shouldn't sleep in bras) . . . or better yet. . . go to bed naked! That always works!

8

Be Spontaneous

Surprise him with a gift here or there or adhere to his love language. Cook him his favorite meal or dessert from time to time. Do adventurous sports and sometimes make reservations to do something outlandish. Even though in his mind he may be like, This girl is crazy, he'll never forget what you-all did, and it'll put a smile on his face that you planned it and surprised him and got him to do something he never thought he'd do, and he actually enjoyed it. Nobody likes a bore. Let me let you in on a little secret about men. Sometimes they test you to see what you'll say. They won't make you go along with it; they simply want to know if you were willing to take the risk with and for them. If he asks you to do something and he knows you're terrified of doing it, then say, "You know I'm scared, but if you want to do it, I'll do it with you." Then, hopefully, he says,

"You don't have to do it, I just wanted to see if you would." If he doesn't . . . that's messed up, but go through with it . . . you'll be okay! For men, there's something about a ride-or-die type of woman. One he can depend on and one he knows always has his back. So be spontaneous and keep him on his toes and surprise him with things you've never done before and be willing to try new things you may not like but will make him happy.

9

Support Him

As we all know, women were built from man's rib cage. The purpose of the rib cage is protection, support, and respiration. The rib cage protects the lungs but also, most importantly, the heart. Women were created to support a man and protect his heart. In any and every situation, you have to support your man. If he falls on hard times . . . support him. If he does something you know is wrong . . . support him in front of others . . . then scold him about it later on at home. If he's feeling unsure of himself . . . encourage him. Not only do you support him, but you help build him up . . . not tear him down. Support can be anything from standing up for him when he's not around to offering to drive halfway to a remote destination to having to hold the bills down to support his goals. He should always feel like he can come to you about anything and that you will listen. That's not to say you don't have a voice. You're able to provide your opinion on things if asked, but sometimes they just need you to listen, just like we do. Always feeling like we have to have a say in something makes men feel we don't trust them enough to make decisions on their own and lead. So support him in his endeavors, and when he asks for your advice or opinion, then willingly give it.

10

Serve Him

I've heard people say, "I'm not making his plate; he's a grown man, he can make it himself." Yes, he is a grown man, and yes, he can make his own plate, but he should feel like a king, and a king gets his food served to him. I should probably make this disclaimer now before I speak on anything else: these things are for a man who is deserving. A man has to be deserving to receive this royal treatment. When making dinner, serve him and the children before serving yourself. When out in public at an event, ask him if he wants you to make his plate before you make your own. Make sure he has something to drink and something to wipe his hands with, and when he's finished, take his plate and napkin and throw it away. If you notice in the middle of the meal that he has finished his drink, ask him if he would like some more.

Serve him sexually. This was mentioned before, but it needs to be mentioned again. If he likes to get kinky and do some outlandish things . . . at least try it out. Be his little sex slave . . .

Make his lunch . . . why have him spending $20 a day for breakfast and lunch when you can make his lunch with the leftover dinner and have that $20 a day going towards house expenses? I can go on and on about ways to serve him, but you get the drift.

11

Ride Or Die

Ladies. . . you have to be a rider! Most of you know what I mean by a rider, but for those who don't, let me define it for you. A rider is someone who supports and stands by her man through anything. She is more loyal to him than his boys are. Look at Bonnie and Clyde; she rode with him until the end . . . literally!

Men are egotistical creatures. What I mean by that is that men like their egos stroked. Men like to know they're appreciated. This may be difficult for some women because we tend to expect men to do certain things, which may be legitimate expectations, but it doesn't mean we shouldn't appreciate them for doing it. For instance, it is expected for a husband to take the trash out in some households. So when they do it, we don't say anything because this is an expectation. But why not? Is it that hard to say, "Oh, thanks for taking the trash out today?" It lets the man know not only that we notice him doing it, but that we appreciate it as well. So stroke his ego, but most importantly, stroke his ego with your loyalty: be a ride-or-die wife! Loyalty is essential to a man. When a man is with a woman who has an affair on him, his ego has been destroyed, and it is not as easy for men to forgive the way women can. So being true and loyal to your husband is most definitely one way to keep him happy. If you feel your loyalty is about to go out of the door, communication is essential to informing him of your needs. When he does something wrong and you know he's dead wrong but people are around, you defend him no matter what! Then, when you get home, tell him, "You know you were wrong." But in public, you stand by him no matter what. You also always stand by him when he's not around. He has to feel and know he can trust you, no matter what! Don't be snitching on him, and don't go against him in public, it's embarrassing. If others are ganging up on him, you take his side . . . always! If something is about to go down, take them heels off, and jump in it! You have to have a partner who is willing to ride for you.

12

Be Domestic

Be domestic, ladies! A man loves a traditional woman who can handle her business outside of the home AND inside of the home. When he comes home, he should come home to a clean home. Wash the dishes, do laundry, fold the clothes, mind the children (with his help), cook dinner, and keep the calendar updated with soccer matches, back-to-school nights, his parents' anniversary, etc. Now, let me clarify: every household divides their responsibilities up differently because some people are better at doing some things better than others. So, if he prefers to cook and you do the dishes, cool! I'm just saying whatever your responsibilities are, make sure you do them and you continuously do them. Always remember to continue doing the same things you did when he met you because those things are a part of what attracted him to you. I don't know a man who wouldn't love to come home from a long day at work to see his wife with some booty shorts on cooking him a hot meal! You might even get some dessert after! Your home is your castle, and it's also a reflection of you, so be sure to keep it clean. As for the children, I hate it when I see a woman out looking cute with her red bottoms on, Chanel bag, Gucci glasses, etc., and her child is with her looking like she hasn't had her hair combed in a week. I don't care if you were rushing out of the house. Then it should be the other way around, the child should be looking flawless, and you should be looking a mess! So, be sure to adhere to your role as a wife and mother.

13

Be > Than Average

Ladies, there are a million and one pretty faces walking around this Earth. How are you different? How do you stand out? What makes your man look at you and say, "Me fooling around is not worth the risk of losing her?" Is it your intelligence? Maybe it's your drive. Is it your sense of humor and chill? Or perhaps how domestic you are? I don't know what it is, but there has to be more substance underneath than just a cute face and a big butt! I like to call those things accessories or the icing on the cake. You see, the icing is the extra goodness you get, but the cake is dense and is the substance. Most people don't just eat a handful of icing; they would rather have it on the cake to balance it out. You have to have substance, too, because beauty will fade, and you better hope you have something else there that keeps him attracted to you. Too many women are focused on what society feels beauty is. Have you ever heard the expression "Beauty is in the eye of the beholder?" This is your man. This is you. You have to be your own beautiful, and beauty is not just a physical attribute. Beauty is both internal and external. Twerking on Instagram will heighten the chances of you getting a man who sees you as a sexual being and nothing more. Don't follow the masses. Be unique, stand out, and be bold, brave, and unwavering.

14

Pick and Choose Your Battles

We've all heard this before, but with men, you have to be careful about the things you choose to argue about because, after a while, men will start calling it nagging. Men hate a nagging woman. This doesn't mean you don't speak up on things that make you upset; just make sure it's something worth arguing about. In time, you'll learn which arguments to take on and which ones to leave alone. In time, you will also learn another way to bring up something or address a need or concern. Not everything that makes you upset needs to be argued about. You can at times wait to bring it up later. Or you can simply ignore it, unless you get to a point where it really bothers you. I think people mistake this to mean you shouldn't voice your opinion or speak your mind, and this is not the case. You should always be able to express your feelings about a particular situation, but

29

it doesn't always have to be in a condescending tone causing an argument. So you should address specific concerns in a variety of ways, each time becoming sterner. Using this approach will avoid an immediate argument because addressing it the first two times in a non-argumentative demeanor and a calm voice won't put him in a defensive stance. By the third time, if the issue is still occurring, now you can say you've addressed it twice and it is still happening, so now we have a bigger issue. Sometimes people feel if they walk away from a situation, then they lost the battle. Well, first of all, you're not in competition with your spouse, you're on the same team. So compromise is key, and thinking before speaking is wise.

15

Have a Sense of Humor

No man wants a dry woman. . . period! He does not want a snooty woman, a woman who can't take a joke, a woman who is always serious and can't enjoy life. Men have enough to deal with at work and in the world. So he wants to be able to come home, have light conversation, and converse, all the while being able to joke around with you. When you-all are out in public, he should be able to laugh with you, and I mean a good hearty laugh. The two of you should be able to look at each other and just laugh. You two should have inside jokes that only you two get. He should be comfortable joking with you about things and not afraid you're going to blow up. In a perfect world, we would have the same sense of humor as our spouse, but that is not always the case. So men when you're married, you should know what you can joke about and what is off limits. Not every woman thinks it's funny when you break your neck to see the body of a woman who just walked past. That's not what this chapter means. Things like that may be off-limits in your relationship, unless the two of you are into that. By a sense of humor I mean, seeing someone or them fall and you laugh because you know they will laugh as well. Or you do something like pass gas really loud because you know she will find it funny as well. So it's important to learn your spouse's sense of humor so you can stay within the guidelines of what to joke about and what to leave alone.

16
Understand His Childhood

Sometimes we get into relationships, and we have certain expectations or preconceived notions of what a man should do. As true as these things may be, guess what ladies . . . your man might not be that man who takes the trash out, and if that is a major issue for you, realize this before the vows are made and run! Or you can express why this is important for you and then understand why he doesn't take the trash out. Yelling at him to take the trash out and calling him "less than a man" is not going to get him to take the trash out. But talking and learning that as a child, he never had to take the trash out because his father always did it can explain his actions. I'm not saying it shouldn't be discussed that this is important for him to do, I'm just saying a person's childhood shapes their entire life. Your childhood influences your future decisions because of learned behavior. With a little discussion, you can begin to understand why he does some of the things he does instead of assuming it's because he doesn't love you or is just being a jerk. Taking time to know his past and understanding before assuming can save you from a lot of arguments. People don't understand how influential your childhood is. It influences your adult decisions. The things we do and say and the way we behave and interact with other people come from our childhood and what was learned. Some things are influenced by our environment, and other things are influenced by the biological aspect of our youth. So it's important to know his family structure. Did he have to drop out of school to work and support his family? Did he watch his mother or father abuse the other one? Did he come from a one or two parent household? What's his culture like? These things are important and should be discussed prior to marriage.

77

Compromise

Every relationship is about compromise, whether it's family, friendship, strictly platonic, or romantic, but most importantly when you're married. There will be some things women can't seem to get their men to do, for whatever reason. This is when you ask yourself, "How important is this? Is this something I'll go to bed angry about and still wake up pissed off?" If so, then you may be passionate about it, and you may not want to budge on it. But if the issue is about something you argue about and realize later you just want to get over it, and you have a slight concern that maybe your approach or tone was wrong or maybe you can now see his point of view, even though you saw it then, but you refused to let him win! Then, you may want to compromise and just let it go, or agree to disagree. Again, pick and choose your battles. Rule of thumb, if it's something that burns you to the core and you know you cannot get over it, then talk about it and come up with a satisfactory result for the both of you. Otherwise, leave it alone. Sometimes in a marriage, you give up on things that you may have cared about, such as getting him to pick up after himself or getting him to do things on your terms. But there should be things you never give up on, such as your goals, dreams, and aspirations. You compromise on the little things, never the big things.

18

Bring Something to the Table

Please don't be that woman who is talking bad about her husband who can't do this or buy you that, when you're not bringing anything to the table for him to want to go that extra mile. How are you complaining that he can't afford that Gucci bag you want for your birthday when you can't even afford to buy it for yourself? You have to be able to bring something else to the table besides a pretty face and a nice body. You want to be a stay-at-home mom while he pays all of the bills, keeps gas in your car and pays for all of the dinner outings? Cool, but make sure you have an education to back you up just in case he falls on hard times—you can get a decent job and pick up the slack—or in case he decides to leave. Don't complain about the kind of car he has because it's fifteen years old and breaks down every other week when you don't even have a car. You have to bring something to the table. Men find a woman more attractive when he knows she can handle her business and can hold her own without him.

19

Be His Homie

Xscape talks about this one in their song, "Just Kickin' It." Men want a woman who is cool. One who he can talk to like he is talking to his boys . . . of course not EXACTLY like he's talking to his boys, but for the most part. I don't care how close you and your husband are; he is NOT discussing everything with you like he would with his boys. But being cool and allowing him to go out without you, whether that's going to the strip club (unless you're passionate about this not happening), going on an all guys trip to Vegas, etc. Let him live! You never want to restrict him too much from doing what he wants, but there are boundaries, and they should be stated up front. There will be times when throughout the relationship, you may have to stress them again. But being that friend who he can confide in and letting him know you got his back regardless of the situation, will allow the relationship to be a more open and transparent relationship, where the two of you can communicate without arguing. Now, having his back regardless of the situation does not include things like staying in an abusive relationship, but forgiving things like infidelity. If you are a woman who can forgive her husband for stepping out, then by all means, forgive him, support your stance, and have his back when your girls want to jump down your throat for not leaving!

20

Give Him Space

I don't think I can stress this enough! Give him SPACE! Every man needs his space to do him and be himself. Sometimes the kids can be a bit unruly and running around like little crazy people. If he's had a hard day at work and he's tired, and you were off for the day or you were working from home, then allow him the opportunity to go into his man cave, shut the door and have some peace and quiet for an hour or so. Then, when he resurfaces, he will be a more tolerable person to be around. We all have those moments when we need some alone time. Space is not only allowing him his alone time, but it's also allowing him to go out without you to hang with his fellas. No man wants to be crowded. So yes, you can have a Netflix-and-chill night, but not every weekend. Also, don't be all up in his business. If you have reason to check his phone, then, by all means, check it, but when you find what you've been lookin' for, don't get upset! But if you don't have a reason to check his phone, you just want to check it for your insecurities, then it's a waste of time. If you have no reason to mistrust him, then don't create one. In time, these urges will pass. When you've been with someone for so long, their phone, email, etc., no longer interests you, because you've matured and then you take on the attitude that if he is doing something, you will find out eventually. Also, it's okay if he has a password on his phone. Sometimes it's not about being sneaky, rather as human beings, we like to have some privacy. I don't think there's anything wrong with being married and having a little independent privacy. For some couples, this may not work; they may not be allowed to have locks on their phones, so you have to state certain things up front and how you feel about them.

21

Be Natural

Now, ladies, there's nothing wrong with getting weave . . . but at least make sure you have edges and hair underneath! Social media nowadays is deceiving. Men aren't stupid. If you've only posted face shots, then the odds are pretty good you may be hiding something . . . maybe you're shaped like Spongebob or a pop tart, I don't know. But be proud of your shape . . . some men would love it! Hiding it isn't the answer, because then, if you meet up with someone who doesn't like the square shape, then your feelings are going to be hurt when you don't hear from him again. The makeup is a problem. No man wants to have to wash his white t-shirt every time he hugs you because you got foundation on his t-shirt, so stop caking it on. A man hates nothing more than when you-all have been dating for a while, then one day he wakes up beside you, and he doesn't recognize you.

A lot of women will sleep in their makeup during the courting and dating stage, but when they become married, they decide to reveal their natural selves, and for some marriages, it causes a problem. I can even recall a man suing his wife because she was ugly and she gave him an ugly child. The woman wore makeup all of the time to hide her looks, so he was unaware of how unattractive she really was until they had a child. Makeup will have you looking like a completely different human being, and it's deceiving and unfair. Men love to know you can wake up and look the same way you looked before going to bed. Again, makeup isn't bad, but overdoing it is.

22
Know His Love Language

Knowing and adhering to his love language is essential. There are five languages of love, and you should check out the book The 5 Love Languages by Gary Chapman. When you know his love language, you're able to fulfill him. The other things mentioned will make him happy. But your love language fulfills you. Your love language is what makes you feel loved and appreciated. It lets you know your spouse has taken the time to listen to your needs. The five love languages are Words of Affirmation (complimenting him), Gifts (self-explanatory), Quality Time (spending alone time with your spouse), Acts of Services (helping your spouse out with tasks), and Physical Touch (touching them, sexual pleasure, holding hands). Not every man's love language is physical touch (although it may seem that way). So making sure you adhere to his love language is vital because you can be doing everything else mentioned above, but if you're not fulfilling him, then he's happy but not fulfilled, and a lack of fulfillment can make him go astray or leave.

23

Leave the Expectations Behind

I made this point the last one for women because it is a very critical one. From since women were little girls, they wanted to play dress-up and house, and they were the moms and whatever little boys were there were the daddies. "Daddy" didn't have to do much but fix things broken, while "Mommy" washed the dishes and cooked. From a young age, this is taught. It's called learned behavior, and it can be learned from the home, a friend's home, the environment, TV, etc. With social media nowadays, the environment is weighing in a lot on perceptions and expectations. But these expectations follow most women into their adulthood, and expectations lead to failure a lot of times. So many women who are in their late twenties get into a new relationship in hopes of becoming a wife. With this preconceived notion, they have a vision of how the "married" life should be . . . but in reality, it doesn't go that way. Women get into marriages with the expectation that he's going to make her happy and he's going to love her, and he won't cheat, and he will take out the trash, and he will help with the kids, and he won't be a slob, etc. But expectations lead to failure because when she expects these things and they don't happen, she becomes upset and he can't understand why. It's because he had an expectation (unbeknownst to him) that he didn't meet. Ladies, stop putting these expectations on these men and then getting upset when he doesn't meet them. We're all different. Without communication, how is he supposed to know what you expect of him? Communication will not only inform him of what you expect of him, but it will let you know if he's going to uphold that expectation because if he can't or simply doesn't want to, he will say that. This way, your expectation can turn from an expectation to a request. You're requesting/asking him to do something, and then you're explaining why you would like for him to do this. This is far better communication than creating an expectation only you know about because you think every man is built the same way. We're all built to be individuals. You can't expect him to love you if you're just not a lovable person anymore. You can't expect him to make you happy; you have to be happy with yourself to be happy. Too many women have fallen for the "idea" of what marriage is, but an idea is just that . . . an idea. You can't marry an idea; you marry a person, a real live human being who has lived a life with a set of different experiences, affirmations, perceptions, and perspectives. You can't go into a marriage 50% and expect him to be 50% so you-all can make 100%. You have to go into the marriage 100%. So he complements you and adds to your wholeness. He then becomes an accessory, extra good who will take you even farther. So, ladies, leave the expectations at the front door of the wedding chapel because they will leave you hurt.

24

Does Chivalry Still Exist?

I bet there are men out there who don't even know the meaning of the word (just kidding)! But seriously . . . it's the ladies turn and men, you-all need to know what it is that makes us tick and what turns us on, and chivalry is a definite turn-on. No, it's not old-school, it's called being raised with manners, and it doesn't matter if you're a thug or a perfect gentleman, chivalry should always be kept in the forefront. You're not a punk. Go around and open her door for her when you're leaving her parents' house or your boys are around. Increasing your pace to grab the door in front of her and holding her at the small of her back while you gently usher her in first, then you go in behind her, that's a protective stance that women adore. If you're in a fancy restaurant and she says she is cold, offer her your suit jacket. If you're driving back from the movies and she mentions she is hungry, offer to stop and get her something to eat. If you know it's late and she says she has no gas in her car, offer to take her car to fill it up because it's late and yes, SOMETIMES you can pay for it, because always asking for her card is a bit annoying, unless her car costs $100 to fill up, then offer to pay occasionally!

A final note on the gas: if you-all are together stopping for gas in her car, then please get out and pump her gas. I mean, it should be automatic because you should be the one in the driver's seat anyway. I'm not saying she can't help you drive if you're going long distances, but regular outings, you should be driving. When you're home chilling watching Monday night football, and you know she just went grocery shopping with the kids, once you hear that garage go up or that door slam, pause the game, put on your slippers and be there to grab the groceries so she can put them away. While you're out there getting the groceries and you see how filthy her car is that she uses all day driving around your kids and wearing every single hat you can think of from soccer mom, teacher, doctor, chef, sex slave, etc., offer (after the game or sometime soon) to take her car to get washed so YOUR wife, who is a reflection of you, looks good when she's driving your kids around the world.

25

She's Not a Man

Men, it is not attractive when you ask us to help you carry that heavy-a** dresser up the stairs, then get upset because we have to keep putting it down because it's heavy. So stop asking us! You need to get on the phone, call your brother, your father, or your boys and ask them to help you move it because she's not a man and she wasn't built to do those types of things. Can she do it? Maybe, but that's not the issue. The problem is when we start to lose sight of our roles. Her role is not to do the strenuous, hard work men do. We were built to be soft with curves, ready to support you, feed you, turn your house into a home, comfort you, bring you peace, satisfy your sexual cravings, etc., not bring dressers up two flights of stairs. Now, ladies, this doesn't mean you can't help with a few things that aren't heavy and some ladies don't mind helping with the heavy things. You do what works for your relationship. But the majority of women feel like you should be calling your boys for that or waiting until one of them or your brother and father comes over and grabbing them for a quick second to help you. Women want to know you know your role and you stick to it and allow her to stick to hers! The same goes for things about her car. When she needs an oil change, when she needs new tires, when something goes wrong with her car, you should be the one handling that. She has enough things to do in the home, with the kids and her career as well, so this should fall in the man's lane.

26
Listen

Every woman wants a man who can listen. A man who understands when his wife wants his opinion, advice, or simply to listen. I know, men aren't mind-readers, and some men haven't quite learned their wives' nonverbal cues, so ladies, starting the conversation off with I just want you to listen will help them do just that. A man who can listen is a man who becomes a friend, and being married to your friend means a lasting relationship. She doesn't need a rebuttal after every statement. She doesn't need you to be waiting for a point to get your word in. She doesn't need you to look for a point where you can become defensive, just listen. All she wants you to do is understand her feelings. She's hurt, and she's expressing it, and if you don't listen, then you don't care. But if you listen, then you will understand she's not trying to persuade you to agree with her.

She's just trying to get you to see her point. She is just trying to get you to understand that regardless of you-all disagreeing, her feelings got hurt and nobody can change that. So for the argument to be solved, you have to acknowledge you hurt her, apologize, and then move on. You don't get to determine when she can or can't be hurt. We are all individuals. Acknowledging her hurt allows her to open up more freely and frequently with you when something is bothering her.

27

Understand Her Body

I'm just going to say it. There is nothing more dissatisfying than a man who doesn't know or understand his woman's body . . . and don't think we don't know. We may not say anything to you, but we know. A woman can tell when a man has experience by the way he moves and by the way he touches her. Women want a man who has some sexual experience (I don't mean one that's slept with two hundred women) so that'll he'll be able to read her body, satisfy and fulfill her. If you don't know how to go down, fellas . . . then please refrain from going down until you either seek lessons from watching it on YouTube or simply ask her how she likes it. We would much rather you tell us you have no experience in that area then waste our time. Some women are willing to teach you how to do what you need to do. Being able to understand her body shows her you care about satisfying her and you're not a selfish lover. Women hate selfish lovers. A selfish lover is a lover who only looks to get his and then he's done. There's no round two, no foreplay, nothing: they get right to the point, get theirs, and they're done. So, you have to try or pray to get yours before he gets his, and this isn't fair. He doesn't give you any kind of foreplay to get you hot and ready, so you have to mentally do it yourself. This is boring and too much work for her. You have to get her in the mood and then do what she likes, so she welcomes it. Show her you care and she will return the favor.

Dr. April V. Martin

28
Loyalty is a Must

You hear it all the time, and there's a reason why women say, "All men are dogs." Some women say that probably every day, and if it's not out of their mouth, then it's in their head. But you ever wonder why a woman says that? It's because she's been hurt a hundred times over by men in her past, and the number one reason is usually infidelity. Most women have been cheated on at least once in their life, and it's a painful experience if you loved that person. But when you've been cheated on over and over and over again, you become angry, and you begin to lose hope in love. So you become either a vengeful female pimp or a Ms. Independent who builds a Great Wall of China to ensure no one can hurt her again. This is why loyalty is so important to women because she's been hurt and humiliated. Her heart and ego have been bruised, and it makes her feel

58

less than what she is worth because sometimes she can be doing everything right, but because he sees something else walk by with a phat a**, he does a one-nighter, she finds out, and she questions herself. Now, she's insecure and checking your phone every night. This can explain why some women don't want to do anything for a man without a ring because it's a possibility that it's going to be for nothing, only making it better for the next woman. That's how the saying goes: "One woman always makes it better for the next one." When you're married, and you commit adultery more than once, and she has forgiven you, and she continues to wash your clothes, fold them, cook you dinner, wash the dishes, do the grocery shopping, handle the finances, keep the kids together, go over the kids' homework, keep the house clean, etc., and you cheat again and again, there's going to be a point where she's had enough. A lot of times, once she leaves and time has elapsed, and you both move on, you move on with someone, and you do things for her you said you would never do and you don't cheat on her. You treat her better than you ever treated the one who loved you more than anyone and did all of the things he asked. Is that fair? So, fellas, be loyal and true or don't say, "I do."

29

Don't be Brand New

A lot of times, men enjoy the chase, so they court you, wine and dine you and do all of these wonderful things to make you fall head over in heels in love with them, only for them to stop doing them once you-all get married. Stop stopping like that, men. You can't be one way before marriage and then switch the game up after you get married. It's called "false advertising." You portrayed yourself to be one way, a caring, affectionate, go-getter, high achiever; then once you get married, you become cold-hearted, selfish, and content. She fell in love with the person she met. By becoming someone else, you've tricked her, and it's a trick that is costing her her life and love. She needs consistency. If you used to go out to eat once a month, then continue to do that. If you used to buy her flowers occasionally just because, then continue to do that. If you used to give her massages after she had a long day at work, then continue to do those things. They spark memories and remind her of how it was then, and it lets her know you still care, the same way you did before.

30
Be Her Friend

A lot of times people tend to start off as friends before a romantic relationship, and once marriage gets in the picture, the friendship usually fades and transforms. Being friends is important. Be her friend to the point she sometimes finds herself saying to you, "Girl!" This means sometimes she forgets when she's speaking to you or her girlfriend. This may feel like an insult to you, but it's not, it's a compliment. It means she feels comfortable when talking to you, the same comfort she feels when talking to her friends. There's no judgment and she can be herself. Is she going to tell you everything she tells her girls? Absolutely not! But she's comfortable enough to tell you things a lot of wives may not tell. Being a friend means, listening, being supportive and encouraging. Being a friend means being there for her when she's at her lowest and her highest. Being a friend means praying for her when she needs it the most, and lending a helping hand. This will allow the relationship to have less drama and continually grow.

31
Be a Great Father

This is an essential point because whether all of your kids are with your current spouse or you have kids with someone else from a previous marriage or relationship, a woman admires a man who is a great father. It shows her that not only are you an excellent provider and a hard worker but you own up to your responsibility, especially if you're coming into the marriage with prior children and your wife doesn't have any. If you aren't a great father, it might hinder her from wanting to have kids with you. Being a great father is also a sign of maturity, which is very attractive to her. So regardless of the situation between you and your baby momma, you should respect her at all times and remember it's all about the child(ren), and it is better to show them you respect her as the mother of your kids than to show them respect is not necessary for their mother and women!

32
Keep Them H*** in Check

Since we're speaking of baby mommas, please
do your wife a favor and keep your baby momma(s)
and ex-girlfriend(s) in check. No, she doesn't need
to be calling you at 1:00 AM if it's not an emergency
about the child's well-being. Your wife comes first,
period! All of the intricate details should be ironed
out before marriage so everyone knows how to
stay in their lanes. If you let some things slide, then
your baby momma will think it's cool. Conversing
daily on matters not involving the child is not
acceptable. Hanging out with your baby momma
is not acceptable. You can pick up the child and
bring them to your home, but going over there to
chill and saying you're just spending time with the
child is not acceptable. You never want your wife
to feel like she's in competition, especially if you-all
haven't had kids yet. Also, please be transparent. If

the baby momma is sending you inappropriate texts or constantly texting you late at night, you better tell your wife, because the last thing you want is for her to find out without you mentioning it. Sneaking is not cool. You have to inform your wife of the conversations that take place, and then it is left for the ex-girlfriend or baby momma and the wife to be a mature, cordial adult and think about the best interest of the child(ren).

33
Be Honest

Sometimes men tend not to say how they truly feel, in fear of hurting their wives' feelings. But she would much rather you be honest with her than having her believe everything is cool. If her cooking is bad, tell her. Maybe she can then start taking lessons or at least try to improve for herself as well as to be able to provide you with good-tasting food. If the love is fading, tell her. Will it hurt her? Sure, but again, honesty is better, so something can be done to try and fix it. If you need sex more often, tell her. Give her an opportunity to make it right. Being honest is always the best policy, regardless of how she may feel. If she does happen to get upset by something you've said, then ask her, Would you rather me lie or not tell you? Nobody likes a liar, and women despise being lied to because then it puts them on guard as to why you're telling lies. So keep it real at all times. She's a big girl, so she'll just have to grow a thicker skin.

34

Be Aggressive

Now, this does not refer to beating your girl. This means every woman wants to know she has a strong man. A man who can dominate her at times and be in control of things. A man is supposed to be the king, therefore, showing a little authority from time to time is appealing. Being a little aggressive in your language or a little vulgar is sexually appetizing to women. Let her know you can take charge. When she walks by in those boy shorts, grab her butt and pull her to you. During sex, be a little rough. She doesn't always want to make love; sometimes she just wants to __ __ __ __ (you can fill in the blanks). A little aggression is very attractive. When you're going to kiss her, hold her face. It shows you have control. Believe it or not, some women even like to be a little defiant on purpose, just so you can flex your muscles. Sometimes the best time to use this aggression is when she's mad at you, and you can just grab her, throw her down, and do what you do . . . she'll forgive you . . . for that night, but she'll be ready to revisit her reason for being mad in the morning.

Dr. April V. Martin

35
Surprise Her

Not every woman likes to be surprised by being thrown a big party, and this is where you have to know your woman. But you can most certainly surprise those who don't like to be surprised by doing something out of the norm for her. If you never ever go to the mall with her, then one day when she's getting dressed to go, tell her you want to go with her. Sometimes you gotta take one for the team. If your wife loves surprises, then have the house staged for a romantic dinner when she gets off of work. Or when you know she's been stressed lately, have your mother take the kids one day and send her to have a spa day; it'll show her you've been paying attention. Speak her love language. If she loves gifts, leave a gift in her lunch box if possible. Or you can do something as simple as leave a handwritten love note in her purse; it'll put a smile on her face. Be sure to spread your surprises out. Doing it too often becomes the norm. But doing it occasionally will have her heart fluttering again.

36
For Christ's Sake, Plan Something

I know you've seen the meme posts about a woman wanting their man to take some initiative and plan something. Again, for women, it's about taking charge and being a man. Woman don't want to always hear, "It's whatever you want to do, babe." Don't you have a mind of your own? Don't think you're doing her a favor by being "compromising." No, she's thinking you're a bore. Plan something on occasion. Be creative, think of unique things to do, and plan the whole outing, whether it be a new dinner spot and a nude spa after, something to show her you're interested in doing things with her and have new and creative ideas to share with her. I know not all men are creative, but it's not hard to google things to do and pick one. She gets tired of always having to think of things to do. Her mind is always thinking about things to do; she has to pick the kids up, pick up the dry cleaning, make the grocery list, pay that daycare payment, buy the kids some shoes, etc. Relieve her by planning something to do and somewhere for the kids to go, so you-all can enjoy each other's company.

57

Business vs. Street

Now, men, this may be difficult for some . . . or a lot of you, because with this one, you either have it or you don't, and by "it," I mean "swag," "style," or whatever you want to call it. A woman loves a man who can handle his business at work. It doesn't matter whether you're a white-collar worker with a paisley tie on and a nice tailored suit or a blue-collar worker with dirty clothes on and dirt underneath the nails of your rough, manly hands. A man who can take that business attire and switch it up by putting on a fitted hat, a white t-shirt, some jeans, and tennis shoes and look like he's never seen a corporate job in his life is so sexy! Or switching from the dirty clothes of a blue-collar worker to the clean business suit. It's something about a man who can switch it up. He can go around the hood and is well respected, yet he can go into a business meeting and do his thing.

We know not every man has street cred, but just the switching up of the outfits is sexy. It means you can go to a high-class gala and blend right in or go to a house party in the hood and have the time of your life. This is so appealing to a woman because it gives her a sense of security. She feels safe, and few things appeal more to a woman than a man who makes her feel safe when she is in his presence. A man who walks into a room and demands attention. A man who has street cred and a successful career is most certainly going to be chased by the women because it is not a common thing. It is usually a bad boy turned good, in the sense of eventually making the right choices in life, maturing and understanding that that "bad" life can only go on for so long and to survive in this world, something more practical has to occur.

38

Stay in Your Lane

We all should know ourselves by now. So please don't be embarrassing, fellas. If you know you don't have an ounce of street in you, please don't go walking in the lounge like a thug, and then a fight breaks out and you running for cover with your wife. Stay in your lane. By all means, you have to protect your wife. If someone is disrespecting her, you have to defend her, and you may lose the fight, but that's okay, you did what you had to do. I mean, don't walk around like you big and bad starting stuff when you know you can't fight. Another thing, fellas, when you're out with your girl and y'all in a lounge chilling, if you know you can't dance, don't dance. It's embarrassing, and it's completely fine just to stand up and nod your head. This also applies to the marriage. If you know you're a terrible cook, then you don't need to offer to cook, you're just going to waste the ingredients you-all spent money on. So if you're lacking in one area, make sure to pick it up in another. There's no need to try and be Mr. Handyman if you know you can't fix anything. Just call someone up to fix it and be done with it. There's no need to try and impress her, it's better to be real with yourself and upfront that this isn't your kind of thing. We know you're human and not all men can fix everything or knows about cars or even sports. So be real with yourself and upfront with her.

39
Be Helpful

A woman loves when a man is willing, on his own, to help his wife out without her having to ask. Women say it all the time to their friends about you: "Why do I always have to ask him to do this? He sees it needs to be done!" If you see her struggling with a million bags and the baby is still in the car, get up and go get the baby out of the car. She shouldn't have to be making multiple trips back and forth while you just sit and watch her. If you see she is not feeling well, and she is doing several things, like laundry, folding clothes, cooking dinner, checking homework, etc., offer to do the homework, something to lighten her load. If you see her car is filthy, offer to take it to get washed. If you know you have just thrown your clothes all over the room and your side is a mess, then pick the clothes up and tidy your side before she has to do it herself or ask you to do it. Women will be willing to do more for you if you show her you're willing to do more for her. By offering your help, you're showing her you not only take the initiative but pay attention to her needs, and that most certainly will not go unnoticed.

40

Support Her

Yes, women were built from the rib of a man to support his heart. But that doesn't mean she doesn't need you to support her too, regardless of how independent she is. Support her dreams and goals and always remind her of her determination and her ambitions. A woman needs to know you have her back. This is important because a lot of times women meet a man and fall in love, they get married, she bears his children, and then her life becomes consumed with being a wife and mother, and she forgets about her dreams and her passions. Before she knows it, she's lost herself, her self-identity, and when she looks in the mirror, she tells herself it's too late now. Do women as mothers and wives make sacrifices? Yes. But it doesn't mean you lose yourself and it is not selfish to say that sometimes you need a break away from the kids to accomplish your goal(s), whether that be going back to school to finish that degree or writing your first book or the journey of entrepreneurship. Either way, you have to always remind her of those dreams and aspirations she had when you first met her, because it is easy for women to forget. This is very important because it shows her you support her goals and never felt she had to give it all up for you or the kids. It becomes a juggling act where you take care of your husband and your kids, and that extra thirty minutes can go towards you completing a homework assignment., writing a paragraph for your book, or submitting a 501(c)(3) application for that business. As her husband, you have to be there to help her reach her goals. Take the kids to their grandparents' house for a few hours so she can concentrate on her business plan. Or tell the kids to leave mommy alone for an hour or two because she has homework to do. Doing these things will avoid her having resentment towards you in the future. Women tend to let resentment build. Why? It's because at a certain point in a woman's life she gets tired of asking you to do the same things over and over again. She gets tired of the arguing, and eventually, she becomes silent. It's a true saying that "when a woman stops arguing with you, then you need to worry." It's because she no longer cares, and that is usually due to one of two reasons: one, she is going to leave you, or two, someone else is occupying her time. So be sure to support her in her endeavors and instead of thinking she's nagging you on certain things, be grateful she is still arguing with you because it shows she still cares.

41

Be Naked

By being naked, I mean be transparent with her. You and your wife are one. You should show her and give her all of you. Hiding your feelings or keeping secrets is no way to be in a marriage. Your partner can't learn to trust you if she feels you're hiding something. When your phone is always turned over, she may feel you're hiding something. When you get antsy every time she asks to see your phone for a second, you watch her every move and as soon as she's done, you're quick to grab it, why? Just think how you would feel if the roles were reversed. Especially as men with egos, you cringe at the thought of your wife keeping a secret because the first thing your mind goes to is infidelity and men can't fathom another man having what's theirs. So why shouldn't she feel the same way? When your woman feels she can trust you, then you don't have to worry about her cracking your phone, nagging you about your whereabouts, or simply not trusting you. When a woman trusts her husband, she will no longer feel the need to question your every move and go through your phone because it becomes too much. So reveal yourself to your spouse. If you can't be your true self to her, then who can you be your true self to?

42

She's #1

There's a verse in the Bible (KJV), Genesis 2:24, that states, "Therefore shall a man leave his father and mother, and shall cleave unto his wife, and they shall be one flesh." This is a powerful verse because it explains the wife's position. She is #1 to him. She should be held higher than anyone because "a man who finds a wife finds a good thing." Some may find this difficult to adhere to, but this is what the Bible states, and it shows the position in which He has put the wife. You should cling to your wife because you-all are one. So when you're around your boys, it's okay to hold her hand, if that's something you normally do, or even if she grabs your hand, hold it. Who are they or anyone else to make you block the love who you have for your wife? Just because you're at a party with a lot of attractive women around, if your wife wants to give you a kiss or show a little public affection, are you really going to turn your head or push her away? If so, why? Because when you get home, she's the one that's going to cook your meal, clean the house, and take care of your kids, so is she not worth a simple public display of affection? It lets her feel comfortable knowing the presence of other people doesn't intimidate you into being someone else. It shows her love is the same whether people are or aren't around. It shows you put her above them. Switching it up just because people are around is not love, and it's embarrassing for your wife. It also makes the outside world feel that you don't love her the way in which you actually may, and perceptions can interfere with a healthy relationship. So always remember she is your winning prize and she should always be treated as such.

43

She Should Never Feel Threatened

We all have a past, and the best thing to do with a past, especially if you have a dirty one, is to be upfront about it. You never want your wife to find out something about your past that you didn't tell her. Again, be transparent because she can't be mad at the fact that you were a pimp or just doing you if you were a single man. I mean, she can be mad, she can feel whatever she wants, but what is she going to do, leave? No, she has to deal with it, but not being completely upfront will create bigger issues. If there was an ex you were in love with, you don't have to tell your wife you were in love with her unless your wife asks, but you should make sure you mention you used to mess with her if you-all see her sometimes. This way the wife isn't blindsided when you're out and she's around. Your wife may not say anything, but nonverbal body language can speak loudly at times. If you see your ex-girlfriend, ex-wife, or an old lover, and she approaches you to talk, and she leans in to give you a hug, and your wife is standing beside you, and you don't introduce her, it's a red flag, and it's disrespectful. Be sure to introduce her as your wife as soon as you finish hugging because now your wife feels threatened by this other woman. Your wife should never feel that another woman, especially an ex you have history with, can walk right in and have a night with her husband. Whether she can or can't, it should never appear that way. When you and your wife are together, she should feel like the only woman in the room.

44

Know Her Love Language

This was mentioned for the women, but it's reemphasized here for the men because you both have love languages that need to be understood by your spouse. Just because she's a woman doesn't mean she is automatically going to have the love language of "quality time" or "gifts." Women can have a love language of physical touch too. When it comes to love languages, you can't assume what theirs is just because they're a man or woman. You have to ask, and then, once you know, you have to be sure to speak it to her. Not speaking her love language will leave her feeling empty and unfulfilled. This is where the happy-yet-unfulfilled part comes in. Ironically enough, as women age, their love language may change to being "physical touch" because when women hit their mid-thirties, their sexual prowess starts and lasts until their forties. While most men's sexual heat tend to decrease the older they get. So don't be surprised if your wife tells you her love language has changed to "physical touch." If this is the case, you better have a plan "B" to be able to satisfy her sexual thirst, because for women this thirst becomes overwhelming. By not fulfilling it, you may be pushing her into the arms of a man who can.

45

Exude Intelligence

Women love intelligence. A woman loves to be able to be stimulated not only physically, but more importantly, mentally. When a man can stimulate a woman's mind, he can be the one to stay for the long haul. Sure, there are a lot of men who can satisfy your sexual needs, but not everyone can stimulate you mentally. You ever know a couple who were long-distance lovers and met online, and they spoke on the phone for months before ever seeing each other in person or hanging out, and they fell madly in love with one another? That's because they were stimulated mentally. You can create a deeper connection when the connection is first mental. Being able to connect with her mentally will make it just easier to satisfy her sexually because she is already in love with your mind. Women can easily find a man who is packing and can satisfy her in the bed but can't speak one intelligent word. It gets old. As women age, we want more from a man than just sex, although it is a significant part; you have to get to her mind. Being able to have both will keep her at home where she needs to be.

46
Let Her Hang

Finally, fellas, I know sometimes you may not like her girlfriends because some of them may be "out there" or because some of her friends are single and you believe birds of a feather flock together. But if you've selected a strong woman, then you know she has her own mind, regardless of what her friends may be doing. Give her the freedom to hang with her girls. As a woman, she does a lot, so she needs to be able to let loose from time to time. As Michele Obama stated, "I love my husband, but my girls are my sanity." Women are emotional beings. They release to their girlfriends: it's innate, and it's their nature. It's not that they're running back to tell their girlfriends about you-all's marriage, they're simply looking for another perspective to see if they were wrong or right. Women talk to one another and can spill how they're feeling to their girlfriends.

Not allowing her that is stifling. She can't possibly come to you about you. So let her hang, have fun, let loose, and enjoy life, all the while maintaining proper balance as a wife, mother, and friend.

I hope this book has implanted at least one new thing you feel can help improve your marriage or relationship. Marriage and relationships is not an easy thing, and if I would have had this book before saying "I do," we would have had a much smoother ride at the beginning of our marriage. If you do decide to adhere to one, some, or all of these secrets, and you notice or don't notice a change in your marriage, please send me feedback. Thanks! info@ draprilmartinspeaks.com.

About the Author

Dr. April V. Martin wants to change the world one book and one speech at a time. As a Certified Relationship Coach, motivational speaker on love and relationships, entrepreneurship, empowerment, and your life purpose, she hopes to instill hope, wisdom, and encouragement into the minds of her readers. Dr. Martin is also the CEO of a nonprofit organization called Achieving Mental Victory, Inc. (AMV). She is an avid supporter of mental health.

Dr. Martin attended Oxon Hill High School, where she was selected to be a part of the "Who's Who Among American High School Students." This is a publication for students who have graduated with a 4.00 GPA. She later attended the University of Maryland, College Park, where she was on the National Dean's List for all four years of college. She has a bachelor's degree in criminal justice and criminology, a master's degree in psychology and a Ph.D. in psychology.

She has been employed with the federal government for 20 years and is currently a realtor as well.

Dr. April V. Martin

Dr. April V. Martin currently resides in Maryland with her husband and three daughters. In her spare time, she enjoys spending time with her family, traveling, reading, writing, and dancing.

Please leave a book review on the website below, and be sure to follow me on Instagram: DrAprilVMartin_Speaker, Facebook: DrAprilVMartin.Speaker, and Twitter: DrAprilVMartin

www.draprilmartinspeaks.com

Acknowledgments

I want to thank my publishing company, Koehler Books, editors, graphic designer, and everyone who had a hand in making this book. You are appreciated. Thank you.